what am i?

A Picture Book of
Rhyming Autumn Riddles

WRITTEN BY SHANA GORIAN
ILLUSTRATED BY A. FYLYPENKO

Written by Shana Gorian
Illustrated by A. Fylypenko aka. ArtPortra

First Edition, 2022

I'm a small, furry mammal
that can climb a tall tree.
With my long, bushy tail,
I'm easy to see.

what am I?

A squirrel.

I grow in a field
from the spring through the fall.
By late in September,
I might be ten feet tall.

what am I?

Corn.

In spring, I am green.

In autumn, I impress.

If you don't rake me up,

your lawn might be a mess.

what am I?

Leaves.

I stand guard all day
like a sailor on deck.
Despite my spooky name,
the crows still peck.

what am I?

A scarecrow.

Beneath an oak tree,
you'll find me on the ground.
Squirrels collect me for food
to eat all year round.

what am I?

An acorn.

My thick shell contains
my pulp and my seeds.
In October each year,
I'm what a front porch needs.

what am I?

A pumpkin.

I grow on a tree,
and I'm yellow, green, or red.
You can bake me in a pie
or just eat me, instead.

what am I?

An apple.

Children ride on my back.

Round in circles we go.

But hold onto my saddle.

I'm not always slow!

What am I?

A pony.

Farmers use me
to harvest a crop.
Children like hayrides
that I pull 'til I stop.

what am I?

A tractor.

I reap a large harvest
throughout the fall.
Children search through my fields
for the best gourd of all.

A pumpkin patch.

I shine like gold,
and I light up the night sky.
When I'm full, I look just
like a big pumpkin pie.

what am I?

A harvest moon.

Wear me when the autumn wind whips through the air. But grab your gloves, scarf, and hat. It's chilly out there!

What am I?

A sweater or jacket.

I'm orange, white, and yellow,
and I taste really sweet.
Kids like to eat me.
I'm considered a treat.

what am I?

Candy corn.

Bake me in the autumn when the leaves fall from the trees. I'm sweet, and I'm crusty, and I always aim to please.

what am I?

A pie.

Now you've guessed all there is.
That's right. You're all done.
So, on to the next book.
Go have some more fun!

What—you've read all your books?
Then go do your chores!
Better yet, go outside and play
in the beautiful outdoors.

Thank you for joining me
in this game about the fall.
Did you get some riddles right?
Just a few? Or, maybe, all?

Shana Gorian is the author of the Rosco the Rascal series, early middle grade novels for kids ages 6-10. She loves holidays and seasons, and she loves to rhyme even when no one is listening.

Look for more seasonal, fun-loving books in the **What Am I?** series for kids

A. Fylypenko is the artist behind the ARTPORTRA brand. Her extensive experience in illustration and design helps her breathe life into the unique concepts brought to her by creative clients from around the world.

Made in the USA
Middletown, DE
03 October 2024

62011067R00020